"Instead she was dodging
this way and that
Racing and chasing
that furry black cat"

DR
With thanks to Ameerah, who was the inspiration
and to her Mummy and Daddy, Anouska and Martyn.

CS
Forever thankful to Raiden, who is not so little anymore.
And a warm thanks to everyone who has ever pushed me to aim for the stars.

ISBN: 978-0-9954736-9-0

Text copyright © Darren Richardson 2017
Illustration copyright © Carmen Stacey 2017

The right of Darren Richardson and Carmen Stacey to be identified as the author and illustrator of this work has been asserted by them in accordance with the Copyright, Designs and Patents Act 1988

All rights reserved. No part of this publication may be reproduced, stored in a retrieval system, or transmitted in any form or by any means (electronic, mechanical, photocopying, recording or otherwise) without the prior written permission of the publisher

Printed in Suffolk by Gipping Press Ltd

Staring out of shop windows, stuck up in the streets
Were bright coloured signs and big coloured sheets
With red-headed clowns and long winding slides
Merry-go-rounds and fast whizzy rides

Ameerah stared out as she knelt on her bed
With her chin in her hands; with a shake of her head
She stared as outside the coloured lights flashed
Loud music crashed, and
the dodgem cars bashed

She had been stuck here all afternoon
Stuck feeling sorry, stuck here in her room
While Mummy was downstairs with Dad's tea to cook
Ameerah was upstairs with her head in a book

She read to her cat and imagined its purr
As she snuggled up tight to the fluffy pink fur
Outside people were laughing out loud
How she wished that she could be part of the crowd

She thought about Daddy and what he would say
She thought of the things that had happened that day
The morning had started without as much as a frown
As she drove with her Mummy to the shops in the town

Together they looked for her school uniform
And a new winter coat that was snuggly and warm
They had gone to the shops with all the school stuff
Bought a pencil case covered in fluffy pink fluff

The roads were so busy with cars rushing past
The pavements full of people walking so fast
But sat on a corner next to a man in a hat
All furry and frightened crouched a very small cat

A cat that was bunched and was hunched on the floor
As black as the little black cat from next door
Ameerah had wanted to cuddle that cat
The cat that was hunched by the man in the hat

While her mum juggled bags and answered the phone
Ameerah stood there for a moment alone
She decided to go give the cat a quick cuddle
While Mummy was talking and in a bit of a muddle

Her Mummy had told her again and again
"Hold hands, Ameerah, don't run off" and then....
With a jolt and a bolt Ameerah shot through the crowd
Ignoring her name being shouted out loud

No matter how hard her Mummy called
Ameerah paid no attention, didn't listen at all
Instead she was dodging this way and that
Racing and chasing that furry black cat

That cat didn't stop as it ran down the street
Dashing through people's legs, dancing over their feet
Ameerah was chasing swooping left, swaying right
Not caring that Mummy was now out of sight

But soon there was no cat for Ameerah to chase
She felt very strange in a very strange place
It seemed very scary in this part of town
And the smile on her face soon turned into a frown

The shops didn't look like the ones that she knew
Where could she be? Just what should she do?
The fun game of chase had turned out all wrong
Oh, where was that cat? Where had Mummy gone?

Her face filled with fear as her eyes filled with tears
And she strained very hard with both of her ears
As hard as she tried she could not hear her name
She could not hear her Mummy, this was not a fun game

All the people around her seemed to be in a rush
One waved to a taxi, some ran for the bus
Nobody noticed her, they were all in a hurry
She felt so alone, and she started to worry

Then through the crowd all dressed in black
Stood a man in a cap with POLICE on his back
Ameerah walked over, she felt very small
And tugged on his trousers, gave them quite a sharp pull

The policeman turned around and said, "What have we here?"
Looked down at Ameerah and seeing her fear,
Swept her up in his arms and in a comforting tone
Added, "Now then young lady, are you all on your own?"

With a sad little silent nod of her head
Ameerah remembered the words her Mummy had said
In the back of her coat a label was sewn
With a name and phone number if she was lost and alone

The policeman looked at the label and dialed
Looked at Ameerah and for the first time he smiled
He spoke on the phone and said, "No need to worry,
Your Mummy is on her way here in a hurry."

Oh, where was her Mummy? When would she be here?
Ameerah was wishing her mum would appear
Peering and poking her head through the crowd
Ameerah could hear her name shouted out loud

Then there was her Mummy with her arms open wide
Ameerah felt safe, felt all warm inside
They cuddled together and hugged like a bear
Until mum lifted her up, right up into the air

"I'm sorry," cried Ameerah, "for chasing the cat
I never should have run off and left you like that"
She felt very safe now her mum squeezed her tight
And told her, "Young lady you gave me a fright."

But then mum gave a look that Ameerah knew well
The look Mummy gave when Dad made a bad smell;
When she ran through the lounge in her wet muddy boots
Or pulled Mummy's flowers, pulled them up by the roots

"How many times have I told you Ameerah?
You must hold my hand, I could not be any clearer
About all the dangers in this part of town;
About nasty strangers; about getting knocked down"

On most of their journeys if given a choice
Mummy would sing at the top of her voice
But this trip was silent, there was no sing-a-long
No waving of hands; not a hint of a song

Now back in her room she heard steps on the stairs
And on the back of her neck she felt prickly hairs
The bedroom door opened and there stood her Dad
But he didn't look angry, he didn't look mad

"Now then young lady you must understand
How important it is to hold Mummy's hand.
So, if you promise that you will not dare
To run off again, you can go to the fair

So, they rode on the dodgems and Mum won a bear
By hitting some coconuts stuck up in the air
They ate candy floss, some got stuck to her face
As she watched the big whirly rides whizz round into space

They shared fizzy orange and a packet of sweets,
Had rides on the merry-go-round as a treat
As for Ameerah, I think we all know
That she held mummy's hand and she didn't let go